INVISIBLE CONVERSATIONS
What we say without Speaking

I0441426

Marlene Green

INVISIBLE CONVERSATIONS

What we say without Speaking

Marlene Green

marlene@marlene-green.com

CONTENTS

INTRODUCTION

I wrote this book with the intention of touching other people's lives – to use my talent to open other people's minds and hearts so that they may live a more fulfilling, healthier, and happier life.

The life we create is our story. We often forget that we have a choice in how we write this story. Some people live their lives without ever realizing what they truly care and love most about this world. One of the main reasons for this is that sometimes we aren't very good at understanding who we are. While we may be really good at what we do, we sometimes don't have a clue about how to control our thoughts or how we come across to the world around us. We can focus so much of our energy and attention on outside events that we can neglect understanding our inner self.

The best way to achieve our goals and learn and grow as individuals is to first understand who we are and how the conversations we have with ourselves can influence what we do. I refer to these conversations as our *invisible conversations*. These are so powerful they can drive us to success or failure. They can impact our persona in a way that can propel us forward, bring us back, or completely stop us.

Our *invisible conversations* entail our inner dialogue of judgments, evaluations, worries, and insecurities. They can make us dwell on the past or worry about the future. Whether we realize it or not we're having these *invisible conversations* while we're interacting with others and it keeps us from being present in the moment and achieving our goals.

This book is a guide to help you understand and become aware of the subconscious conversations you have about yourself or others that stand in the way of your success. Once you begin to understand your *invisible conversations*, you can change them, and start taking control of your thoughts and not have your thoughts control you.

The book is divided into seven sections, each with an exercise to help you work on the overall mosaic of *invisible conversations*. The sections are simple and easy to follow, but they require practice and a willingness to understand more about who you are and how you come across to the world around you.

I trust this book will serve as a great guide to achieving your goals and understanding your inner self.

Remember, believe in yourself and you will accomplish your dreams!

marlene@marlene-green.com

"Some people think they are concentrating when they're merely worrying"
~Bobby Jones, Golf Legend

FOCUS

Focus is the ability to stay directed on a path and work towards a vision that you care about and are committed to fulfill.

When you go through life without any set goals in mind, you wake up day after day with no sense of drive or accomplishment. Whatever happens is the luck of the draw – you are totally at the mercy of life and what it puts on your path. However, when you have a dream, a clear plan, and smaller goals to achieve that dream along the way, you can then begin to focus all your energy on achieving your dream and accomplishing what you are most passionate about. This will, without a doubt, bring a great sense of meaning and accomplishment to your life.

Many people live their lives without being aware that they can choose the life they want to lead. This realization, while simple in nature has changed the lives of millions. One day, after following the path that was laid in front of them, they realize that their heart, soul, and mind are not fulfilled; that they are living a life without color, passion, or joy. They wake up and say, "It's time to take a risk and try something new." And they go for it, and from that day on, their lives are changed forever.

It is valuable to know yourself and realize who you are and what you really care about. Sometimes you get so busy with everything around you that you lose perspective on what you really love. Before going any further, take a moment to close your eyes and shut out everything around you, and think about the following questions:

What do you truly love? What are your life's dreams? How do you plan to achieve them?

A big step to achieving your goals is to have a clear plan. Writing it down will make it a lot easier to follow. It will help you stay focused and not yield to the inner or outer voices that are filled with worries, fears, and doubts.

Take out a notepad, and write something next to each of the above questions. Visualize your answers as clearly as you can. Your goals can be anything from working out twice a week, beginning a healthy diet, getting a new client, developing a strategy for your company, or simply taking a risk and seeing where it leads you. What's important is to just choose one and go for it.

Often times, the abundance of ideas in your head seem so overwhelming that you end up doing nothing. There are so many choices and so many directions to go that you find yourself unable to choose any single one of them. You may also have the belief that if you choose to focus on one goal, then you'll be neglecting other things you care about or that you'll make the wrong choice and end up spending a lot of time and energy on something you'll later regret.

The first step in overcoming this situation is to challenge that belief. If you spend your whole live afraid to choose something in fear of neglecting other things you care about or not making the right choice, your whole life will pass by and you'll end up missing many wonderful opportunities.

From the list of goals you created, choose one and just focus on it completely for a couple of minutes. Forget about everything else for a moment.

Would accomplishing this goal be meaningful to you? Will it bring you happiness?

If so, make this your weekly goal. Focus on it during the week, work on it during the day, enjoy the process, and see what happens! Results will come if you begin to focus. Sometimes writing your weekly goal in a place you'll constantly see will help remind you in case you forget or lose focus. For some people, writing in a journal works really well. Having a journal also allows you to track your progress and remind yourself of what is really meaningful to you.

While you begin to work on your goals, remember it is important to get into the habit of choosing one goal and sticking to it until you achieve an outcome. If you don't have goals and if you don't

marlene@marlene-green.com

have anything to focus on, life will take over. You will not be in the driver's seat of life. You'll be no more than a passenger heading in an unknown direction. You can't always stop what comes your way, but you can control how you handle it.

Try to let go of those thoughts or *invisible conversations* in your head that keep you from achieving what you want to do in life. If you hold on to those negative thoughts, tomorrow will be the same. You can only create a new future by adopting a new way of doing things. If you start with a clean slate today, you can create a different future for tomorrow. If you just keep holding on to the past you'll just carry the same problems forward and you'll be living the same life over and over again.

If you start creating goals based on what you care about, you work to achieve them, and you stay focused, you will be surprised at what magic is unleashed in you and will begin to learn what makes you unique and what lights you up inside.

It is natural that when you first start working on your goals, you might encounter some resistance. It's hard for people to break their habits, or change things they've done repeatedly over the years. When you start working on your goal, be present with it and be aware of the resistance you may encounter. When your *invisible conversations* **the little voice in your head,** tells you that you can't do it, you're not good enough, or it's too hard, just acknowledge it, thank it for sharing, and move on. Remember, stay with your goal. Always be actively pursuing it. If you become too passive, the obstacles will find it easier to stop you from achieving your goals.

Reaction is one of the biggest challenges in staying focused on your goals. It is the easiest way to stray from being present. Reaction could manifest itself in the form of worry or fear. Choosing your goal, and staying focused and committed takes practice. Remember, identify your negative *invisible conversations,* acknowledge them, and continue on. I know you can do it.

I recently worked with a client who had a hard time focusing. Choosing one thing made her feel like she was choosing favorites and neglecting all the other goals she cared about. Her day spun out of control and she accomplished less. Most of us can identify with this situation. "Should I pursue this, or work on that? Should I start this, or finish that?" When you go into this mode, you only waste time being indecisive and don't accomplish much.

I worked with my client until we came up with a plan of action. The first step was to prioritize all her "cares." The next step was to make promises against her cares with a timeline as well as set her conditions of satisfaction. Every day she focused on her plan until the practice became part of her life. To this day, she is thriving because of that simple realization that she needed to make promises to work on her goals, set dates for them, and establish conditions of satisfaction.

The lesson here is that choosing one goal does not mean you are ignoring all your other goals. It just means that you are prioritizing and learning to focus on your goals to achieve success.

Before you go any further, take some more time to understand how to tackle obstacles or resistance that you'll meet along the way. Most people are good at setting goals and sketching a quick plan of how to achieve them. However, one of the biggest reasons people don't achieve what they set out to do is because they don't account or prepare for detours they may find along the way. Encountering an unplanned detour will most likely cause you to react, and this will take you off your game. For instance, take something you frequently experience – you're happily driving to work when all of a sudden you see that the road ahead is closed or completely jammed with traffic. You immediately turn to reaction. You get upset, yell at the traffic, or even get into a bad mood from it. Why? Because you've been detoured from your usual route which forces you to step out of your comfort zone and find a different and often unfamiliar way. The same is true with achieving your goals. Almost always, there will be detours from your ideal plan. This may cause you to react very quickly and then focus on what you're reacting to instead of your goal.

Start noticing when you're in reaction. I call it "pushing your buttons" or "grabbing you." You're working on what you care about, and from nowhere a curve ball comes directly at you and you react. The easiest way to know if you're in reaction is by identifying the physical signs when reaction sets in. A natural physical reaction is to tense up. When this happens, pause what you're doing and work on bringing yourself back to the present. Identify what caused you to react. **Don't let your *invisible conversation* take over.** Think for a few minutes about your current situation with your goal in mind, and try to come up with a different route or way of getting there. Instead of seeing this as a negative obstacle, think of it as an interesting challenge. Get creative! Who knows, you might end up finding a route that's even better that the one you planned!

You often miss a lot of opportunities when you overreact to obstacles. Even worse, when you react, you often cause others to react around you. This is because reacting to reaction is very common among people. For instance, one of your friends reacts to something you did and maybe shouts at you for something that wasn't your fault. As a result, you automatically start reacting to their reaction and scream back at them. Then, before you know it, both of you are screaming at each other when it was all just a big misunderstanding. The best thing you can do when you're exposed to reaction either from yourself or someone else is to try to stop as soon as you can. Reaction will make you do things you later regret. Trust me, it's not worth it. This is the time to take a deep breath and ask, "Why am I reacting? STOP!" Pause what you're doing, take a deep breath, and go back to being present. Stay focused on the goal.

I work with Principals of schools. One of the main things we focus on is becoming aware of how their personal lives can have an impact at work. If they had a fight with their spouse in the morning, for example, they might have gone to the school in reaction mode and this would have carried on as a chain reaction: *My husband was angry with me, so I acted angry at the teachers. Then the teachers acted angry with the students, so the students go home sad and may be unmotivated to come back to school the next day.* If that principal had been focused on identifying when she switched into reaction mode, had paused, and then come back to a present or balanced state, many people that day would have been affected differently.

Worry is another obstacle you might encounter along the way. It is one of the *invisible conversations* that stop you from focusing on what's important. It can be a very strong and negative emotion accompanied by fear, anxiety, and trouble. Worry usually makes your mind wander into the past or the future, so it detracts you from staying present. It can completely take you off your game. There is nothing productive about worry. When you're worried and upset and things are bothering you, you're off focus.

Remember you're in control of yourself.

When you become worried, just like reaction, pause and ask yourself if your worry is helping you in any way or if it is just an unjustifiable fear that you can overcome.

When you make a commitment to pursuing a dream or goal, your *invisible conversations* may tell you that *you can't do it, that it's not working, or that you're not good enough.* Don't listen to it! It wants to cause you to worry and be negative. Stop! Look at what you care about, focus, and be in action towards your 'cares' and not your reaction.

Be in charge of your *invisible conversations*. Know which ones support you and which ones stop you.

I invite you to take this opportunity to practice being focused and overcoming worry and reaction. Make an effort to really look at what's important to you. I promise you, it will make a huge difference in your life.

Putting it into practice

- Take a few minutes to write down everything you care about. Keep adding to that list whenever you think of something new. From that list, choose one thing that stands out. This will be your daily goal for the next few weeks.
- Start with 10 minutes every day and just focus on your breathing while you visualize your goal. Once you see what you want to achieve clearly, start visualizing how you're going to get there. This could be anything from a plan, a strategy, or simply smaller checkpoints along the way. As the week goes on, try to increase this time until your goal and your plan to achieve this goal become very clear in your mind.

- Share your idea with your trusted community. Share with them what your goal is and how committed you are to fulfilling this goal. You'll be surprised how many good things come from sharing. You might even discover that the people you find dearest have very similar goals!

- If you find obstacles along the way such as worries or reactions, practice going through the technique we covered in this chapter. Stop what you're doing, pause, take a few deep breaths, remind yourself of your goal, and try to find a new and, if possible, creative way of getting around the obstacle.

- Lastly, track your progress in a notebook or sheet of paper. You'll be proud of how much you accomplish and it'll give you something to look forward to each day!

- If you achieve your goal, build on that confidence and try tackling even bigger goals. When you feel ready, go for your dream!

*"Boundaries emerge from deep within, deep inside of us.
They are connected to letting go of guilt and shame, and to
changing our beliefs about what we deserve. As our thinking
about this becomes clearer, so will our boundaries."*
~Melody Beattie, Author

BOUNDARIES

Boundaries are the limits or borders set by your inner voice that guide you and tell you what you deserve, how you should be treated, and how you should treat others. Part of establishing boundaries is knowing how far to go and how far to allow someone else to go. Did you ever meet someone, and after just a few minutes you knew you shouldn't take the relationship any further? They never said a word and yet you just knew? Sometime our boundaries don't resonate with others and so we immediately feel this way.

While most boundaries are emotional, there are physical boundaries as well. I was in a networking meeting not long ago speaking to a man that was so close to me that there was no space between us. I kept stepping back to try to make more space for myself, but he only kept moving forward, closing that gap. Finally, I just had to push him a bit and make him realize that he was so close to me I was feeling suffocated.

Each one of us, often unaware, sets our own physical boundary wherever we go. When this boundary is crossed, we may feel irritated or simply uncomfortable. Reaction, as we discussed in the Focus and Goal Setting chapter, can quickly take place when boundaries are overstepped.

What do you allow, and what don't you? What do you feel you can have, and what stops you from having it? What do you care about, and what do you feel you deserve?

One of my clients realized that she spent too many hours trying to please others. What drove her was her desire to be loved. When she stopped and looked at what she really cared about, she saw that she had neglected loving herself. When I helped her get in touch with her own 'care' she was able to create boundaries around her that supported who she was, and what she needed as a person.

marlene@marlene-green.com

What bothers you or has you feeling overwhelmed, used, or just plain exhausted? What lights you up and gives you energy? Focus on your standards and how you want to be treated. How do you treat others? Do you respect their boundaries? Do you even know what is important to them? Become focused on learning your boundaries and become open to what others are telling you.

A client shared with me that she had never been good at setting boundaries, but it was something she really wanted to work on. It was more important than ever because at this time she was going through a divorce and her boundaries were being tested. Her thought process was very common; she didn't want to be seen as a bad person who was disrespectful or rude.

I pointed out to her that the best place to start if she wanted to be stronger was to get really clear on what was important to her and what she cared about most in the area of boundaries. She soon realized that she had the power to focus on things that she could have control over during that most difficult time. I helped her commit to something she really cared about and over time she managed to develop full control over it.

For those people who know about divorce or have been affected by it, you know that this is a very difficult place to be in. Sometimes, however, being in this place allows you to really think about what you care about, and what you love in life.

What's important to you? How do you want to create your life? How have boundaries gotten in the way? What are the boundaries that get stepped on by people who don't support you or are actively trying to block your way? What are the boundaries that are important to you?

Look at your world. Listen to your inner voice. What are the boundaries that have helped you go forward or have stopped you? Often the strongest boundaries get formed at a young age. They can become so strong that they can influence how you act to this day. Take a moment to reflect on the boundaries that may have been formed. Are there things you were told when you were young that make you feel like you don't deserve to have everything, achieve your full potential, or simply pursue your life's dreams?

Maybe you were one of the lucky people who grew up without any fears or insecurities and you walked into the world filled with dreams, and then something happened that left you with doubts about yourself and your abilities. Why did that event change how you act and feel? How did that lead you to develop your insecurities or fears about achieving what you most want in your life?

Perhaps some of the negative boundaries were formed from people telling you: "Oh no. You can't do that. You're too old. You didn't have the right education. You're not fit enough." Perhaps you internalized them so completely that now they act as blocks preventing you from achieving your life's goals.

When you allow someone to step on you emotionally, or you feel they're not supporting you, what does that say about your self-respect? Where is the graciousness and self-awareness in every one of us so we may each have a life we love and want?

I had a client who had plans to really reach for the stars. She had a sound marketing plan and was on her way to success. I had just met her and started working with her around the time when she had been advised by a marketing consultant to create a visual picture of what it would look like to achieve her goals, and then, to write it on paper.

I remember our conversation. She was so excited. She really knew she could accomplish all of this, and she presented her wonderful, beautiful dream to her soon-to-be husband. After she explained her dream, her fiancé – for whatever reason – felt like she could not do it, and told her very directly. The spark and excitement that she had inside her just a few seconds before suddenly died with his pessimistic words.

The next day, she called me in tears. Her mood and emotion were close to despair. She allowed her fiancé to take all her pleasure and self-confidence away by not establishing boundaries. One person was given the authority to end her dream and make her think that she did not deserve it.

I received a call years later from this same client to let me know that she was beginning to work on her dream again. She shared with me that while it was tough, over time, she was able to learn from that experience and realize that she needed to set stronger boundaries for herself and not be influenced by others. What her fiancé had told her years ago had stopped her from pursuing her dream only because her boundaries were not strong. Her *invisible conversation* was: "You can say anything you want and I'll believe you because I don't believe in myself." Now, however, she knows that loving herself and having boundaries is just part of achieving her dreams.

Putting it into practice

- Begin to observe when you feel someone has entered a place that is off limits without your permission, and is imposing his or her opinions and judgments on you.

- Start observing when you enter territories without permission and notice how it shows up in your body and mood. Also observe how it affects people around you.

- What are your boundaries with yourself? Know when and how to say no. Practice as much as needed.

- Take responsibility for how you allow others to treat you. Practice recognizing when their behavior towards you is not acceptable.

- When you set a boundary, let go of the outcome. Having boundaries is about loving yourself, not receiving approval.

"It is only shallow people who do not judge by appearance."
~Oscar Wilde, American Novelist

APPEARANCE

Before I begin to tell you about appearance, I'd like to share a little bit more about myself.

My profession as an Image Coach focused mainly on a person's appearance. I coached my clients to become aware of and create non-verbal messages. I worked with groups of people through seminars and workshops, as well as in one-on-one sessions, to develop their perception and power over their non-verbal communication.

During that period, I was a contributing writer and did before-and-after makeovers for Glamour magazine and published a few articles in Vogue. I also appeared on local and national TV shows. I was the Chicago expert on dressing for success.

My before-and-after makeovers turned out so well that I was asked to be on the Jenny Jones show. When I gave Jenny a makeover on national TV, the change was so remarkable that they retained my services as her wardrobe stylist. My talent was discovered and that brought with it several other TV shows and further opportunities to work with famous personalities.

The important thing I learned, having the privilege of working in TV and with people in public positions, is that **the way you look makes a big difference:** how you dress, how you carry yourself, and what your body language communicates is all part of your overall appearance, and ultimately, how the world perceives you.

Appearance is being conscious of the small subtle details that make the difference in how you look and how you present yourself to the world around you. Good grooming habits, clothes that fit correctly, as well as a positive attitude are just some of the components to pay attention to. It is all about presenting your *best* self.

If you wake up in the morning and feel bad about yourself and dress and act accordingly, you will undoubtedly give the impression that

marlene@marlene-green.com

you want to be left alone and not bothered. Alternatively, if you find yourself in a low mood but you wear your nicest clothes and show off your biggest smile, you will still have a positive impact around you. Be in control of your mood and don't let your mood be in control of you!

It's important to realize that your appearance is not shallow. It is a really important element of the message you deliver. Research shows that up to 95% of the way you come across is through your non-verbal conversation. You need to focus on how you want people to see you and this requires a conscious effort.

First lets begin by focusing on the message you want to deliver. The components to consider are what you care about, how you want to be seen, and if you're coming across the way you believe you are. I suggest you begin to develop this awareness. You want to find out if the way others think you are coming across is consistent with how you think you are coming across. The end goal is to find out how and in what ways you can improve what is already wonderful about you. Resist the temptation to make judgments. This exercise is simply a synergy check about how you project yourself, nothing more. Don't be afraid to open the doors. Remember, **knowledge is power**.

While appearance is largely thought of as purely physical, it does not only encompass our image but our mood, our emotions, and our body language as well. It is not only how others see you, but it is also how you see yourself. If you see yourself as a capable, powerful, and trustworthy person you will come across that way. On the other hand if you see yourself as inept, resigned, or having low confidence, then that is how people will treat you.

Wolfgang von Goethe wrote, "If I accept you as you are, I'll make you worse. However, if I treat you as though you are what you are capable of becoming, I help you become that."

A client I worked with last year wanted to talk about relationships at work with trusted friends. He was having difficulties confronting situations that didn't go as planned. He would skirt around issues and never mention that he was upset. He wanted to share his feelings, but at the same time, he didn't want to hurt his relationships. This led him to avoid conversations he needed to have in order to move forward, which in turn created a lot of frustrations and resentments.

My client's biggest question to me was how to handle these situations. As I pointed out to him, the key was to find a midpoint between avoiding someone altogether and being confronting about an issue. I suggested that the best thing was to be honest about his feelings and express his expectations of his co-workers as well as ask for their expectations of him.

When you make a promise and you fulfill it, you establish trust. Trust takes time, but it is a very important part of how people present themselves to others. Standing up for what you need or want is important as well, but as long as it is respectful of others.

What message does your appearance give? Does your appearance project your best self? What is that positive first impression you want to make when you first meet someone? For example if you want to be perceived as happy, a simple smile or an expression of enthusiasm can make all the difference. Smiling is an expression that projects openness and approachability. You'd be surprised how easily you can influence the moods of others by simply smiling. Even if the day at work is not going well, smile at others around you. You never know how much you could cheer up a co-worker and improve the atmosphere in your workplace.

When our life is organized, it is easier to clear our mind or focus on what is really important. When you have a lot of inner noise or clutter, it can cause you to feel overwhelmed. If you are not organized, it is almost impossible to appear to be efficient at what you do and exercise a leadership presence. Think about it, would you trust or do business with someone who is disheveled and appears to be all over the place?

Are you attracting the kind of people and life you want? Ask yourself the following important questions and reflect on the answers you provide.

Who are my communities? Who are my friends? Who are my clients? Who are my colleagues? What is my lifestyle like?

Do your answers portray the life that you want? What do you see that you would like to change? What would you like to keep? What is the common thread? Analyze this as if it were not your life story, but a story you can create in any way that you want. How your 'outer self' reflects your 'inner self' is an important part of attracting the life you want and the people you want to be with.

As I mentioned earlier in the chapter, two other important aspects of appearance are your mood and body language. Check yourself in the mirror: Do you stand tall or are you slouching over? Are your arms folded or open to people? Are your facial expressions inviting, joyous, and exciting, or are you projecting someone who is depressed or unhappy? Each of these elements in addition to several others make up your overall appearance.

There's an exercise I like to have my clients try when concentrating on appearance. One day when you have some time, go through your closet and make piles. Make one pile for the things you love and wear, another for the things you love but which need small changes, and finally, a third for the things you don't wear at all. Cleaning out your closet is like cleaning out your brain. Get rid of the excess – things you don't need or are not working in your life so that new things can come in – the new things that are important to you and represent who you are today. Try it, you'll have fun with it, and you'll have a lot more space when you're done.

When you start with a new inventory every morning, you can consciously begin to decide how you want to project in the world and how you want to be seen.

Now that your closet represents who you are and all the things you love, what story does it tell? Does your closet support the life you are creating? Is there anything missing? Are you comfortable with the way you are dressed? Do you feel like your clothes support the message you are delivering? You will find yourself in many settings throughout your life. Be conscious of each of these settings and how you want to present yourself in each one. If you want to be low key, choose quiet colors and patterns. If you want to stand out, choose brighter colors and creative styles.

What's important is to live a healthy life, to be conscious of what your *invisible conversations* are, and to be aware that there is support everywhere. Remember what appearance means. It's deeper than looking good. If you were looking for a broker, an insurance agent, or a doctor, what are the things you would look for in these people? If any of these professionals appeared unprofessional, unclean, or disorganized in their appearance it would speak volumes about how they conduct themselves and their business. After all, nobody wants to go to a dentist with dirty fingernails!

Examine your non-verbal communication from leadership presence to relationships. Don't be afraid to ask people about what message you're delivering and how you project yourself. Take that courageous step.

As a close to this chapter, I'd love to share a quote by Dr. B. Lown: "Only those who see the invisible can do the impossible."

Putting it into practice

- What presence do you want to project? Are you attracting the kind of people, both personally and professionally, that you want in your life?

- Ask trusted friends or colleagues what your presence projects. What does your body language say about you? What is your usual mood or disposition according to others? See if what they say fits with how you think you come across. If these don't match, what corrections do you need to make?

- Check in with yourself. Does your outer self reflect who you are on the inside?

- What is the message you are sending based on how you dress and groom yourself? Are you aware of the subtleties you project?

- Whenever you find a chance, give the closet exercise a try. You'll have a lot of fun doing it and you'll have a lot more space when you're done.

"We must build a new world; a far better world. One in which the eternal dignity of man is respected."
~Harry Truman, 33rd US President

SOCIAL GRACES

Social graces are the skills and behaviors used to interact in social situations as well as the ability to help people feel comfortable around you. They are very subtle forms of behavior but they can have a strong effect on others. The art of knowing how to use social graces involves paying attention to and knowing the social rules of the places and situations you encounter, as well as being nice and kind to others.

The topic of social graces is very dear to my heart. I truly believe that if you are simply nice and kind to others, if you pay attention to small details, and you stay focused on the present, you will by definition be socially graceful.

It is important to be mindful of your social graces because sometimes your actions can come across differently from what you intend. For instance, let's say you are speaking with someone at a networking function without giving them your full attention because you are looking around the room to see who else is there, or you are at a meeting and you are nervously shaking your leg. You may not mean anything by it, but the message others pick up is "Let's get this over with."

From a social perspective, the message you want to deliver is that you are warm, attentive, and interested in what others have to contribute. It is not fun to be the recipient of the person rolling their eyes, shaking their leg, or acting uninterested. Keep in mind that the people you are not respectful of are human beings often trying to do their best.

Lets begin with the practice of not reacting from the chapter on Focus. This is a powerful vehicle for social graces. Think of Gandhi, Nelson Mandela, and Mother Teresa. What do they all have in common? We admire them because we know they were incredibly grounded and respectful human beings regardless of the situation they encountered in life.

Boundaries also intertwine with social graces. There is timing in knowing when to enter a conversation and when not to interrupt. As time goes on, we all learn that there is an appropriate way to act. There is spatial boundary regarding how close to get to someone when you are speaking with him or her. If you are so close you could kiss, then you are too close!

Listening and being alert are part of good manners as well. When you enter a new environment, whether it is someone's home, office, country, or city, there are new rules to observe if you just listen and watch. For example, pay attention to the clues about when and where to sit when you walk into a person's office for the first time. Similarly, if you invite someone into your office, be aware that it is up to you to make your visitor feel comfortable. Listen consciously so you don't interrupt.

When someone seems to be indifferent to you or you feel they treat you in an unkind manner, take a deep breath and stop yourself from reacting. Their behavior might have nothing to do with you. Whatever you do, it is important you remain respectful. Their reaction is not personal. Sometimes people are preoccupied and it has nothing to do with you. If you stay calm and grounded you may find out what you thought was happening is not at all what is happening. Start exercising self-awareness and see if you do this to others.

You know when you get upset with someone and secretly ignore him or her but no one else is aware of what you're doing? You walk into a person's house and say hello to everyone except that person? Or you are at a meeting and you don't really feel like that person is worthwhile, so you speak about him or her behind their back? When they are around, you are polite to them, but when they are not around you undermine them through gossip or other behavior?

The only person that behavior is going to hurt is you. It will hurt your respect and dignity. Every one of us is connected to each other, so be aware of how your actions impact other people.

Etiquette, manners, and social graces may change depending on the environment, culture and rules of your surroundings. When you don't know the rules, be open to learning. Many times we're not open to learning. We walk into a situation and feel awkward or upset and then get defensive. Our whole body becomes tense and closed up. Inside we're curled up in a ball because were not comfortable. We feel insecure but others may perceive us as defensive and unapproachable.

My friend asked a close friend of hers if she and I could stay with her for a few days in Italy. I wasn't sure what the arrangement was so we gave her a call and politely asked her. I found out that my friend and I were to pay for the housekeeper and cook while we were there. It was perfect. I felt comfortable, knew the rules and had a wonderful time. Again, there are different rules for different occasions. Just ask!

Recently I was at a company meeting where no one was making eye contact. The leader who invited me was so gracious and helped me to feel so comfortable that it lightened up the whole situation. Her way of setting up our communication changed the mood and emotion of everyone present. The meeting could have gone a very different way, but she took control of the situation by being aware, focused, and polite with everyone who attended. We had a great meeting with very open communication.

A dinner party is another occasion where being warm and inviting is important. Of course we all want the food to be perfect, but it is even more important to make the guests feel welcome. After the party is over, the guests won't care if the sweet potatoes were a bit overcooked or not, but they'll care and remember whether it was a warm, fun and loving environment.

Remember the goal is to create an engaging atmosphere that leaves people wanting to come back. When someone spills red wine or breaks an important dish, they feel badly about it, but they feel far worse if you make a big deal out of the accident. If you are afraid of red wine, don't serve it. If you're worried about your china plates, don't use them. Think and practice graciousness. The goal is to create a good experience for everyone and enjoy each other's company.

When you attend a party, it is up to you to be present and engaging. Remember the most important contribution you can give is your best self. It's hard to think of a better time at a party than when everyone is laughing and feels like they're part of the group.

To be really gracious is to treat people with dignity. So if they use the wrong fork, the wrong plate, or the wrong glass, so what? Take care of your own manners. Don't make others wrong with your knowledge. There are times when you can correct others and times when it is inappropriate; be aware of the situation and others feelings. Common sense is part of the equation.

Not reacting in a social situation is so important that I'd like to give you another example. I was developing a seminar and had retained the services of a colleague to assist me. We were clear about the expectations, the price, pretty much everything that would be involved for services rendered. Suddenly, out of nowhere my colleague mentioned that she would like her work copyrighted with her name on every slide of the presentation.

Naturally I was surprised and upset. I panicked about how to approach the situation. This was a friend of mine and I couldn't believe she was changing the terms and demanding that her name be on every piece of material prepared for the seminar. My *invisible conversation* went something like this: "How could she do this to me? What should I do?"

When I was more in control of my reaction, I called her. We spoke about it in a calm and open way. Her reasoning was simple – she merely wanted to be able to use the materials for her own programs, which was understandable and fine with me. No problem! What could have happened if we both went into reaction mode and became defensive? A valuable personal and professional relationship could have been lost. Remember: just ask! But be sure to do it in an open and calm way.

I believe these stories demonstrate that when you don't react, everyone has the opportunity to say what is on their mind. Can you imagine going through life with everyone giving each other the space to be who they want to be? Practice pure graciousness.

When you are open, you can discuss anything and work out almost any situation. It is only when you fail to give people space – when you assume you know what they are thinking and the motives behind their thoughts – that you attack. It causes drama. Treat others around you as you would like others to treat you. The golden rule always works.

If you're in reaction most of the time, you don't even see the person in front of you. You don't even see the situation. You're in reaction mode and everyone wants to run away from you. No one wants to be around that. You need to stop, pause, look at the situation, and then respond appropriately. When you are in reaction you are not present. You are in your head reacting to the *invisible conversations* that have nothing to do with reality. An example would be: something happens to you that you took as an insult and you stay with it all day. Your reaction is the mood you're in and it creates an energy that affects everything you do.

Just a few seconds can make the difference between appearing calm and focused, and creating a whirlwind around you. How about the times when you're running late to a meeting? Your energy can get so hyper that it is like a whirlwind that disrupts everything around you. If you take 5 seconds to stop and pause, it can make all the difference between being perceived as graceful and focused or disorganized and hyper.

I suggest that you ask 5 people how you project yourself to them. If someone said to you, "I think you're fabulous but you're always in a rush," you could ask, "Do you feel like I'm present with you? How does it make you feel when I don't seem to be paying attention to you?"

You'll learn so much by doing this exercise. When you do this, you can begin to look in the mirror and start working on the things you want to change. You're a human being and not perfect. Becoming defensive never works. I've tried it. I've been there. I've done that. It never works. However, being open absolutely works. Kindness? Yes, without question. Who doesn't like being around a kind person? Cheering? Yes. Shouting? No. Pushing? No. Being a guest in someone's home and respecting what's important to him or her? Yes.

I remember many Thanksgiving dinners where the table was set beautifully and the food was exquisite but the hostess was over anxious about everything turning out perfect. Her anxiety was taken out on the guests so no one was comfortable. She forgot that Thanksgiving dinner is about gratitude and love for your life and others. It isn't the material things or even creating the perfect ambience. It's how you treat people. It's how you stop and say, "Happy Thanksgiving. I'm so happy to be sharing this with you." That's what really matters.

Yes, it matters if you have good table manners. However, do you think that if you ate your bread on the wrong plate, at the end of the day it would matter? I suppose if you made a big deal about it, felt uptight, and said, "Well that's wrong;" then it matters. However, if you laugh and say, "I just learned something new. Thank you so much everybody," then it would be fun and no one would get hurt.

When you find that you're not in the best of moods at holiday parties, at work, during phone calls, or whenever you are with other people, remember that everything you do can influence others. Take a few moments to pause and get back to a more balanced state where you can present yourself in a good light to others. Show kindness and patience with the people around you and always appreciate what you have.

Try to remember this at all times – Be respectful of yourself, your friends, your family, your neighbors, your colleagues, and even the people that you barely know like the lady that helps you bag your things at the grocery store. You never know what wonderful things can happen.

Putting it into practice

- Share kind words and opinions of others with people around you.

- Write nice notes expressing kind thoughts and opinions. It is always a good feeling to receive a positive note.

- Reflect on the conversations you have when you walk into a room. What can you learn from these? Do you know how to put people at ease?

 marlene@marlene-green.com

- When you enter someone's home or office, wait and let them take the lead. When you have guests in your home or at your office, take the lead in inviting them to feel welcome.
- Reflect on what it means to be gracious. What can you do to convey this?
- When you are speaking with someone, remember to project in a kind way. Don't let your eyes wander. Give them your 100% complete and undivided attention.

"As we let our light shine, we unconsciously give other people permission to do the same. As we are liberated from our own fear, our presence automatically liberates others."
~Marianne Williamson,
Internationally acclaimed Author and Speaker

PRESENCE

Presence is the state of mindfulness and awareness of yourself and others in your surroundings. It is so broad that it encompasses how you hold your body, the inflections in your voice, your posture, your attitude – in essence, how you present yourself to others. It is also the way you convey your mood when you speak and the way in which you speak.

When you feel that someone is listening to you and aware of you, you get a sense that they are present. Presence is being here, not talking to someone and multi tasking at the same time. Have you ever been on the phone with someone whom you know is doing two things at the same time and not really with you?

Being present is about caring, carefully listening to, and being interested in others. While it may seem hard at first, being present simply involves living in the now. This is a discipline that takes practice and conscious thinking. When done successfully, however, it opens up enormous opportunities that you might have missed otherwise. We cannot connect with people around us unless we are completely present. We have to let go of our thoughts and history, and truly listen through the lens of now.

I worked with a client who was also an Image Consultant. Her specialty was creating an image that was consistent with what the person cared about. She was a master at "imaging others." She taught her clients the importance of projecting a consistent image of themselves on the inside and outside. It was very interesting to get to know this client and see how effective and present she was with her clients at work, and yet how when it came to connecting with herself outside of her work, she was pretty much clueless. Her own image was scattered and uncertain, and she had trouble making decisions and always second-guessed herself.

One of the clues that showed me that she was not present was

 marlene@marlene-green.com

when she spoke she closed her eyes or looked up. I identified how she went into her head and left the present. Through practice, we worked on ways to remain present throughout the day. After working with her, she seemed much more confident and connected to herself as well as others. By staying focused, it kept her out of her *invisible conversations* and much more connected to people around her.

Take a deep breath. Welcome today and know that you can be present by staying aware of your inner voice and thoughts and bringing yourself back to the now whenever your mind begins to wander. There are clues that we can look for to help us know that we're no longer present. When we go into our head, we start thinking we are not good enough, our hearts are pounding, we go into judgment, our bodies tighten... all these are signs that our *invisible conversations* are taking us away. We have power over this, the work is to recognize when it happens and come back to the present

In the coaching world, we call it mood body disposition: it is the state of mind we find ourselves in which influences how we view life and interact with others. The practice is observing ourselves when we are with others and making sure our commitment to staying present is more important then our conversations we have about them. It is our responsibility to observe our habits and make sure we are consistently present so others feel welcomed around us. Being present opens new doors we can't even imagine. People around us will experience the space of openness and feel more comfortable connecting with us. We will experience true awareness, which will allow us to make thoughtful and positive choices in our life. Resignation, bitterness, and resentment are just some of the common moods we may encounter during the day and which resist our presence. However, with practice, we can choose to turn them around and instead, be filled with joy, gratefulness and the drive to achieve our dreams.

The key is to remember that we have a choice. You have little control over what comes your way, but you have a choice about how you react to each situation. No matter how good or bad things are, **you always have a choice** about how you react to them. Staying focused and connected requires being present, and this, in turn, creates your inner power.

People can perceive your presence. They can hear it in the tone of your voice, in your choice of words, in the way you carry your body, and in your facial expressions.

I want you to understand the distinction between presence and reaction. I had a client that paid a dear price for not knowing the difference. The cost was so great that even with all her talents she could not reach success.

My client was a very bright, talented, and beautiful woman who did incredible work. She was respected for her talent but her mood and attitude got in her way. Her low self esteem and confidence caused her to doubt herself and react to situations, keeping her out of the present and in her negative *invisible conversation.*She felt everything around her was her fault. At times she felt like she wasn't good enough, and when she got praised for her work she could only hold the compliment for a few minutes before she negated it in her mind. Her lack of confidence kept her out of the present, constantly dwelling into the past and worrying about the future. However, the way she appeared to the outside world was very different then how she appeared in her head. The conversation that others had about her was that she was intimidating, hard to please, and yet when she was present, she was fun to be with. Her up and down moods had people distrust her and she couldn't figure out what was going on. She had a great job, she was a hard worker, and yet she wasn't getting promoted.

We worked on her conversations, inside and outside, but mainly about staying present and not buying into her assessments of herself. Every morning she meditated. At first it was one minute and then slowly it increased. If she saw that she was reacting to a situation and going into her inner thoughts, she learned to stop, pause, breathe, and come back to the present. The more she did this the more she saw that the way she was thinking and the poor judgments she had of herself, were causing her to fail. As she learned to stay in the now, her presence changed. People began to perceive her as down to earth, grounded, easy to work with, and lovely to be around; a truly positive and generative being.

When we allow ourselves to get wrapped in our heads and not be present, we miss out on so much of what is going on.

This next example is equally as powerful. I had a client who started a company and hired a young person with whom she didn't get along. They were constantly fighting in public. At that time the economy was tough and their business was struggling, so they blamed the tough economic times for their current financial situation. One day, they looked at each other and realized that it wasn't the economy that was affecting the business – it was their interactions and attitude that were affecting the company. They were so wrapped up in their heads about previous situations and the anger they held for each other that they were living the "yesterday" and the history between them. They were not accepting of each other, which did not allow either one of them to be fully present at the company.

They couldn't create a shared commitment because they were more committed to being right than making the business flourish. In doing so, they were not welcoming the ideas of others, which in turn stopped the business from growing. There was no compassion for each other and all they wanted was to get their way and be right to the end.

Being present to a situation is to put whatever history or anger you might have behind, to heal the wounds and let go of resentment, and to get back to the more important goal: to create a successful business, treat your employees well, and be present to each other's possibilities. Only then, when you listen to each other, can your company become aligned in a shared future.

Their constant fighting and arguing affected other people around the company and created a hostile atmosphere. It wasn't a welcoming place. It didn't foster an environment that encouraged innovation. It didn't create a workspace where people thought, "I love being at work. Boy, this is fun and invigorating!" Instead, it caused a great deal of anxiety and doubt. "Who wants to deal with these people? Who needs this in their life?"

Take a moment to reflect on the impact you have on other people. Are you present to their possibilities or do you constantly have inner dialogue and judgment? Practice staying centered, especially when you notice yourself getting off balance.

Be gentle. We're human beings, we make mistakes. Be generous. Be patient. Everyone is good at some things and not as good at others. Acknowledge this and share it with others. They might have qualities you don't have and you will have qualities that they don't have. Give and be generous.

Be open. You want everybody to win. I believe that if one human being is left out, we're all left out. We're all on this planet together; we're all on the same team. Let's support one another; let's support one another to be great. As you begin to exercise these virtues − patience, kindness, and openness − it will become part of your presence and others will notice it and admire it right away. They'll say, "Wow! What a trustworthy person! He or she is generous and kind, open to receiving support as well as willing to help out. Wow! That makes me feel good!" You can't do this if you are in your head. Presence and balance in your life allows you to blend with others and connect in the now.

You'll be surprised at how much other people enjoy helping and guiding you if you're just open to receiving their help. I know personally, it makes me feel great to be able to contribute to another human being's life. You need to be aware that there are times or situations when people don't want to be helped. If that's the case, you can just say, "I respect that you need your space right now, but know that I'm here to help whenever you need it."

Empower people; don't take power from them, give it to them. Know how to look someone in the eyes. Know how to embrace someone without saying one word or even touching him or her.

Have an attitude that is consistent with your emotions. If you're not having a good day, don't be afraid to say it. Otherwise, people may think something is wrong and could even perceive it as being their fault. Do you know how many times people feel bad about something they think they did wrong just to find out a couple of weeks later that it had nothing to do with them? Be open. When you don't feel well, tell others, "You know what? I'm not in a good mood today, so if I'm acting a little off, it's just because I'm not feeling quite like myself." Sometimes, this simple acknowledgement can make all the difference.

Other elements of presence are generosity, consideration, and being in touch with your own emotions.

We all have good qualities and we all have things we need to work on. We all have opportunities and we all have challenges. Acknowledge what you do well and work to do it even better. Don't be afraid to tackle your challenges and turn them into strengths. This is a sure way to make the most of who you are, which in turn, will allow you to fully appreciate your life.

Let go of grudges. Long-held grudges can affect you more than you can imagine. They can take over your mood and your overall presence with others. Be mindful of this. Forgive yourself and others whenever you can. If it is something that will take more time, acknowledge your feelings and say, "You know what? I still hold a grudge against this person, but it's not good for me. It makes me have negative feelings and affects my mood toward everything. For now, I'll put it aside and carry on my life in a cheerful way."

One of the hardest things to do is to embrace being vulnerable. It takes more courage than you think. Embrace it. Embrace your strengths and embrace your weaknesses. Say, **"I love myself!"**

When you want to make an impact and you don't feel that you're making it, look around and see what's missing. Be willing to do what it takes. Do you have the courage to have strength in your convictions? Do you have the courage to say when something is not working?

Do you have the courage to explore yourself? This is important. If you do the hard work you need to do, you'll find out who you are. When I began to explore and develop myself, it was the hardest thing I ever did. Once I discovered the obstacles that stopped me, I was able to embrace them and no longer feel defensive about what I used to think were flaws. The result? **Freedom!**

Don't let your ego get in the way and cause you to react. I promise you, when you go into reaction, you will always regret it. When you're focused, you establish good boundaries, you're graceful, you're present, you're generous, you have courage and a sense of humor, and you believe in what you're doing, **everything is possible.**

Create an environment that not only allows people to contribute, but one that is not all about you. Let it be about them. Give them credit; share with others.

Putting it into practice

- Learn to see yourself as others see you. Your mood, your energy, and your essence are very much a part of your presence.
- Pay attention to how present you are when you are with other people.
- Practice being in the moment and catch yourself when you lose focus.
- Reflect on who you spend time with. Are you attracting the kind of people you want in your life?
- Stay focused on the big picture.
- Stay in control of your actions.
- Ask yourself: am I being proactive?
- Think about the energy you are showing people.

*"The best way to waste your life is by taking notes.
The easiest way to avoid living is to just watch.
Look for the details. Report. Don't participate."*
~Chuck Palahniuk, American Novelist and Journalist

CONNECTION

Connection is about awareness, focus, and consciousness with yourself and with others.

I was recently given the opportunity to coach a renowned scientist. She is young, beautiful, and brilliant. She confessed to me that her work had the potential to touch all of mankind. During our telephone coaching session I could tell how extraordinarily passionate she was about her work. I learned a great deal from her, but during our 30-minute conversation, she never stopped talking. She might as well not have been on the phone with me.

At the end of the conversation, I asked her: "Why are you retaining my services?" She replied, "Because I want my leadership presence to be greater. When I speak in front of people, I want to be able to connect with them. I want to have a greater presence in not only the way I look, but the way I come across."

I then asked her, "Do you know how long you were speaking?" She replied, "No." I said, "Well, it was about 30 minutes, and during that whole time, you never paused to connect with me in any way. You didn't check in with me to see if I was with you and if I understood what you were saying."

We had a great chuckle about it. I gave her exercises to practice connecting with others. One of the exercises was to start being aware of her connection with herself. I told her to practice breathing and taking pauses to stay present. I also gave her an exercise to try to connect with as many people as she could on her ride that day on the 'tube' (British for subway).

When I spoke to her a few days later, she said, "I'm sure the people on the tube thought I was about to have an asthma attack, but I don't care. I just kept breathing in and breathing out and breathing in and it was so exciting to actually look at people and make a conscious effort to connect with them."

Sometimes the subtlest signs can reveal whether you're connecting with someone else or not. The easiest way to tell if you're not connecting with someone is if you don't make good eye contact. I feel negated when I'm talking to someone and he or she doesn't look at me.

It takes just a few seconds to connect. Make eye contact, ask questions, and be mindful of whether you are lost in your *invisible conversations* or you are present to the situation?

Ask yourself: What color are the person's eyes? Are they smiling? What kind of mood are they in? Are they saying, "Yes, yes, yes, yes," but really not connected to you? Are you trying to connect with people when you talk to them, or do you just speak to them to have someone hear you speak?

Look at your communities to see where you are connected and feel comfortable. The best way to begin is to join organizations that you are interested in and want to participate in. You can start with your religious or spiritual affiliations, your gym, or simply the neighborhood in which you live in. Connection is the key to fulfilling your goals and staying positive. We all need support and communities to share our dreams.

Next time you say hello to someone, go out of your way to connect with him or her. Make eye contact, smile. You will be surprised at what can happen when you simply make a gesture to connect with others around you.

Putting it into practice

- What can you do? What skills do you need so you can connect better with each and every person you meet? When you go to a networking meeting, when you walk into an interview, when you are meeting somebody for the first time, what will help you stay connected to others and be present in the situation?

- Be clear on who your inner circle is, and the connections you have to people you trust and who support you. You cannot do everything alone.

- Have a system of follow-up and follow-through for those that you want to develop a closer and stronger relationship with.

- Invite people into your life to get to know them better. Show an interest in them and what they care about.

- Think of ways to show those closest to you how much you care and appreciate them. Then do it. Beautiful things will happen.

"Inaction breeds doubt and fear. Action breeds confidence and courage. If you want to conquer fear, do not sit home and think about it. Go out and get busy."
~Dale Carnegie, Motivational Speaker

COURAGE AND SENSE OF HUMOR

Why did I put Courage and Sense of Humor together? I believe when you do something courageous, it is scary. You don't know what's going to happen. Your heart pounds, your palms sweat. The more you are willing to take a risk and take chances, the more you are open to compliments and criticism. This can be scary. If you make a mistake and take it too seriously you will most likely never step out and take a risk again. You need to have the ability to laugh about your mistakes and have a sense of humor about yourself and others. So it takes courage. It takes courage to be out there. It takes courage to take chances. With a sense of humor, you can laugh at yourself at the end of the day and say, "Wow! What a difference!"

Have you ever noticed that when you are afraid to do something and procrastinate, it becomes harder and harder for you to do it? You just sit there and you are paralyzed with fear? But when you do take action you begin to forget what you're afraid of because you are in the present and no longer focused on the fear?

Courage is a practice. It is a practice of taking chances. It is a practice to be out there and get thick skinned. If you make a mistake, go out there again. Some of the best entrepreneurs are successful because they are determined to accomplish their dream, no matter how many times people tell them "No, you can't do it" or "You're not good enough." They go out there anyway with courage and a sense of humor to learn form their mistakes.

Recently I worked with a colleague in Amsterdam. We had a great program prepared and everything was going as planned, except we never had a chance to practice together! We just thought, "Oh, we can do it." To be honest though, I was scared to death. I could feel my heart beating. I was wondering if it was going to work. By the time I realized we should have practiced more, it was too late. We presented our program, which lasted an hour and a half (although it seemed much longer at the time) and, because we hadn't practiced, it didn't go as well as it could have. It wasn't exactly a disaster, but it wasn't great. Neither of us really trusted each other's process or had confidence that what needed to be done was actually going to get done.

We finished the program and afterwards read the evaluations. They weren't terrible, but they also weren't fabulous. At first we thought to ourselves, "Oh my gosh! Look at these evaluations!" Although most of the ratings were average, we were both accustomed to receiving outstanding feedback. We just couldn't take it. All we wanted to do was run away. As days passed, we continued to look at the evaluations again and again, and we continued to learn something from them. In the end, it was a very valuable learning experience. We learned the importance of practicing and how it's okay to not always be perfect. We had a big laugh about it. Whenever we talk about it, we still get a good kick from it.

To our surprise, out of many presenters that day, we were among the ones that got some of the better ratings. Even though my partner and I hadn't practiced together, we each gave it our best shot. We had the courage to do it, and then we had a sense of humor to accept our mistakes and learn from them.

If you are perfect all the time, how can you learn? And if you don't have the courage to try something new, how do you know whether or not you can do it? Courage and sense of humor are complementary.

I'll give you another example. I had a client who is a marvelous person, intelligent and successful. When he was doing something he already knew how to do and was good at, he was fearless. But when he attempted something new, something he might not be good at, the inner voice in his head would never stop. This is when he needed to find his courage. His weakness was that when he was with people, he wasn't really present with them at all; he was with himself, his own judgments, and his own evaluations. I gave him an exercise to start looking at and trying to interact with people in the audience during his lectures rather than getting caught up in his head and lecturing to himself. His assignment was to connect as much as he could with these people.

He told me that at first he felt terribly uncomfortable doing the exercise. It took a lot of courage for him to change his ways in order to be receptive to the audience and turn the lecture into a dialogue instead of a monologue directed at his listeners. He later thanked me for the work we did for he started connecting with the audience and enjoying his lectures even more than he had before.

Whatever you are working on, there is always an easy part and a difficult part for you. It doesn't take courage to do the easy part. It takes courage to do the difficult part, and even more courage to accept your mistakes and try again and again until you succeed.

Our *invisible conversations* should be about bringing out the best in us. You need to take those conversations and examine them. Don't be afraid to challenge the negative messages they are sending. If you don't examine your negative invisible conversations, you will continue to be afraid and give power to those negative messages.

When you begin to examine the way you look at life and acknowledge that the negative conversations are not helping you achieve your goals, you will become active. When you take that step, you view the world through a different lens. This is how you see new perspectives in life. This is how you get a raise. This is how you get a promotion. This is how you become a team leader – by **growing**.

During some of my seminars, I encounter people who remain quiet the whole time. It makes me wonder if I'm truly reaching them. They may have something to contribute to the group, but are too shy to participate. Everybody misses out. Take a risk! Say what's on your mind. You never know what might come from sharing your thoughts and ideas with others.

Begin to face your fears. What holds you back from expressing yourself at your job or in life? These are the things that take courage to change. Unless you are willing to face those fears, they will continue to stop you. But, once you do challenge them, new openings will follow.

We all like to be with people who are open to laughter. It's no fun being around people who are always defensive or serious. At the slightest suggestion they may be wrong, they explode, "I'm not wrong! I am absolutely right! You don't know what you're talking about!" That is when their defensiveness stops conversations. When that happens, you need to know how to not to let it affect or hurt you personally. Instead, ask yourself aloud, "Hmm, maybe I am wrong. Let's talk about it." Laughter is a great relief and creates openness between people. It allows us to have space between our fears and our reaction to our fears. When you're afraid, think of something funny about the situation and give yourself a good laugh. Believe me, it is much better to laugh than to get defensive and closed.

Part of having courage is letting go of your ego. You have to take risks and not worry about what people think. Know your strengths and your weaknesses. Embrace them both. Practice having humor about your flaws, lighten up – you're only human.

Be willing to take a risk and tell people, "I am taking a risk. I am nervous about it, but I am going to try anyway." Try it and see what happens when you take a chance on something that doesn't come easy for you. Remember: **have courage – you can do it!**

Putting it into practice

- Take a risk. Find one thing that is challenging for you this week and take a risk!

- Know when to quit. If you are on a path and it is not working, or a relationship is not working, know when to change gears.

- Have an attitude that nothing is over your head. Don't be afraid to get your hands dirty.

- Create an environment that allows people to contribute. It takes great courage to make sure it is not all just about you.

- Don't be afraid to dream. See if it is a viable dream, do your homework, practice visualizing it as reality, and decide if it is something you can fully commit to.

CONCLUSION

I hope this book served as a great guide to understanding more about yourself and how you can achieve your dreams.

Remember, the life you create is your story, and you can choose how to write this story. Follow the exercises in this book as much as you can, be kind to others, be open to learning and growing, and I promise you wonderful things will come.

Be conscious of your thoughts. When the negative voice pops in your head that tells you "you can't do it," just smile and say, "thanks, but I actually *can* do it."

Now go out and pursue your dream!

Thank you for allowing me to share this book with you.

In warm regards and appreciation,

Marlene Green

www.ingramcontent.com/pod-product-compliance
Lightning Source LLC
Chambersburg PA
CBHW071302280526
45788CB00004B/1811